Literacy Consultants
DAVID BOOTH • KATHLEEN GOULD LUNDY

Social Studies Consultant
PETER PAPPAS

A Harcourt Achieve Imprint

10801 N. Mopac Expressway
Building # 3
Austin, TX 78759
1.800.531.5015

Steck-Vaughn is a trademark of Harcourt Achieve Inc. registered in the United
States of America and/or other jurisdictions. All inquiries should be mailed to:
Paralegal Department, 6277 Sea Harbor Drive, Orlando, FL 32887.

Ru'bicon © 2007 Rubicon Publishing Inc.
www. rubiconpublishing.com

Project Editor: Kim Koh
Editor: Vicki Low
Editorial Assistants: Caitlin Drake, Joyce Thian
Art Director: Jen Harvey
Project Designer: Jan-John Rivera

7 8 9 10 11   5 4 3 2 1

Escape from East Berlin
ISBN 13: 978-1-4190-3222-6
ISBN 10:   1-4190-3222-4

Printed in Singapore

PHOTO CREDITS: Shutterstock: 2–5, 13, 21, 29, 37, 45–47; istockphoto:
4; The Granger Collection, New York: 4, 13, 29, 45–47; Corbis: 21, 37

ESCAPE FROM EAST BERLIN

Written by
GLEN DOWNEY

Illustrated by
LEO LINGAS
Assistants
MICHAEL GLIDEWELL
LUKE BILBROUGH

HANS KAPPEL

JOHN F. KENNEDY

MARTA KAPPEL

CAROLINE KAPPEL

JAKOB KEITL

REAL PEOPLE IN HISTORY

JOHN F. KENNEDY (1917–1963): President of the United States from 1961–1963. He visited West Berlin in 1963.

WILLY BRANDT (1913–1992): Mayor of West Berlin from 1957–1966. He tried hard to reunite families that had been separated by the Berlin Wall.

FICTIONAL CHARACTERS

HANS KAPPEL: An 11-year-old boy who overhears President Kennedy's speech and yearns for the freedom of West Berlin.

MARTA KAPPEL: Hans's nine-year-old sister. She shows her courage during the escape attempt.

CAROLINE KAPPEL: The mother of Hans and Marta. She risks all to ensure freedom for her family.

JAKOB KEITL: The East German border guard whose mission is to hunt down those who wish to escape East Berlin.

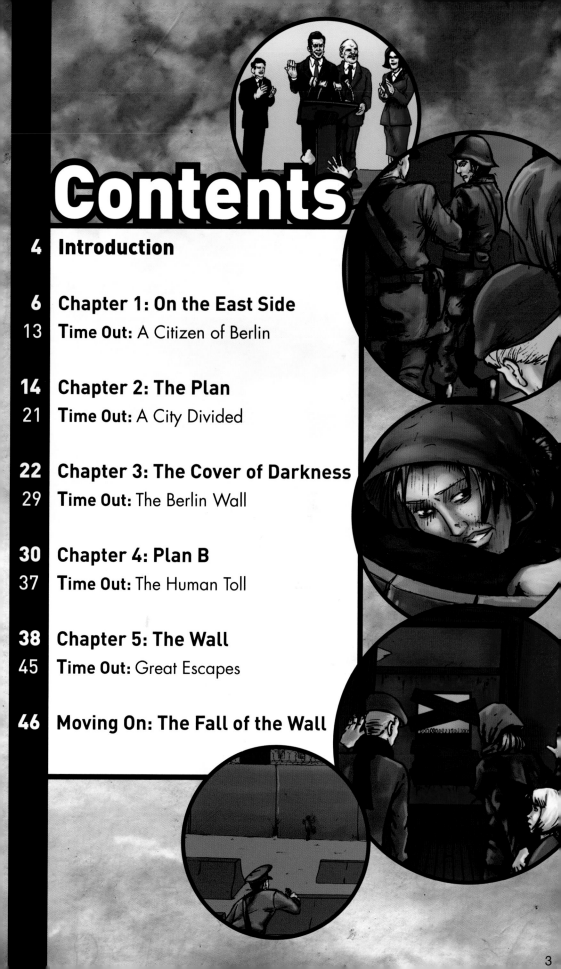

Contents

Children at the Berlin Wall, 1964

At the end of World War II, the United States and the Soviet Union, who had been allies in the war, became enemies in a conflict called the "Cold War." This conflict had no direct fighting, but it created rivalry between the democratic nations, led by the U.S., and communist Soviet Union.

TIMELINE

1945 >>	1948 >>	1949 >>	1961 >>	1962 >>
World War II ends. Germany is divided into four zones. It is occupied by American, British, and French forces in the west and Soviet forces in the east.	West Berlin is blockaded by the Soviets. The Berlin Airlift begins.	The Berlin Airlift ends as the blockade is lifted.	Construction begins on the Berlin Wall.	Peter Fechter is shot to death as he tries to scale the Berlin Wall.

At the center of this conflict was Germany. After its defeat in World War II, Germany was divided up and controlled by Britain, France, the United States, and the Soviet Union. Germany's capital city, Berlin, was also divided up. The western part of Berlin was controlled by the Western nations, while the eastern part of the city was controlled by the Soviets. At first, people were allowed to move freely between West and East Berlin, but this stopped when the Berlin Wall was put up. Those who wanted to escape East Berlin for the freedom of the West had to get over it somehow ...

This story is about the fate of a family from East Berlin who tried to escape.

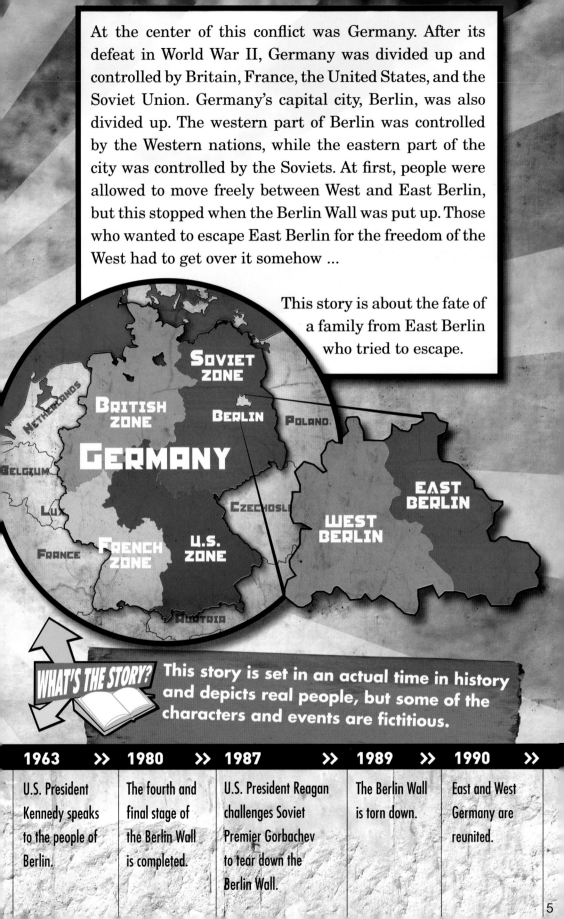

SOVIET ZONE

BRITISH ZONE

BERLIN

POLAND

NETHERLANDS

GERMANY

BELGIUM

LUX

CZECHOSL

FRANCE

FRENCH ZONE

U.S. ZONE

AUSTRIA

EAST BERLIN

WEST BERLIN

WHAT'S THE STORY? This story is set in an actual time in history and depicts real people, but some of the characters and events are fictitious.

1963	1980	1987	1989	1990
U.S. President Kennedy speaks to the people of Berlin.	The fourth and final stage of the Berlin Wall is completed.	U.S. President Reagan challenges Soviet Premier Gorbachev to tear down the Berlin Wall.	The Berlin Wall is torn down.	East and West Germany are reunited.

A CITIZEN OF BERLIN

TIME OUT!

A crowd of 120,000 gathered to listen to President Kennedy when he spoke to the people of West Berlin on June 26, 1963. Here is part of his speech:

Freedom is indivisible, and when one man is enslaved, all are not free.

When all are free, then we can look forward to that day when this city will be joined as one and this country and this great continent of Europe in a peaceful and hopeful globe.

When that day finally comes, as it will, the people of West Berlin can take sober satisfaction in the fact that they were in the front lines for almost two decades.

All free men, wherever they may live, are citizens of Berlin, and therefore, as a free man, I take pride in the words Ich bin ein Berliner (I am a citizen of Berlin).

President Kennedy in West Berlin, 1963

13

TWO WEEKS LATER ...

CHILDREN, I WANT TO SAY SOMETHING IMPORTANT.

WHAT IS IT, MOTHER?

YOU HAVE TO PROMISE ME YOU WILL KEEP IT A SECRET.

I PROMISE, MOTHER.

OH, GOODY. I LIKE SECRETS.

THIS IS NOT A GAME, MARTA. IT'S VERY, VERY SERIOUS.

DO YOU UNDERSTAND THAT?

UH ... YES, MOTHER.

WE'RE LEAVING HOME TOMORROW NIGHT.

WE'RE GOING TO ESCAPE FROM EAST BERLIN.

A CITY DIVIDED

East Berlin, 1945

The Soviets took control of East Berlin in 1945 and imposed their communist system of government. This meant that freedom of speech, freedom of the press, and the right to strike were no longer allowed. People in West Berlin continued to have these rights.

People in East Berlin frequently crossed over to West Berlin to shop and work. In 1948, the Soviets tried to stop this by closing roads and railways into West Berlin. The U.S., Britain, and France began to fly food and supplies directly into West Berlin. The Berlin Airlift was so successful that the Soviets removed the blockade.

By the summer of 1961, the economy of East Berlin was in trouble. Many people who lived there continued to work and shop in West Berlin. On the night of August 13, 1961, the Soviets began building a wall to prevent East Berliners from leaving. Soldiers were ordered to shoot anyone who tried to escape.

THE KAPPELS WONDER IF THEY WILL BE ABLE TO GET PAST THE GUARDS.

THOSE GUARDS ARE ARMED. HOW WILL WE GET BY THEM?

I KNOW.

MARTA, NO!

COME BACK!

WHAT ARE YOU DOING HERE, LITTLE GIRL?

WAAH ... I WANT MY MOMMY!

WHAT IS SHE DOING?

NO, WAIT!

I'M GOING AFTER HER.

23

Berlin Wall guard, 1964

TIME OUT!

Potsdamer Platz

Straße am Potsdamer Bhf.

THE BERLIN WALL

- The Berlin Wall was built several yards into East Berlin. This was done so that West Berlin would not have a reason to knock it down.

- The Wall was first built of chain fencing, barbed wire, concrete blocks, and even boarded-up buildings. In the final phase of the Wall, 45,000 pieces of reinforced concrete were added.

- The Wall was 95 miles long (27 miles of it separated East and West Berlin).

- Checkpoint Charlie was one of three crossing points between East and West Germany. It is a symbol of the Cold War.

- Ten thousand guards watched over the Wall.

CHAPTER 4: PLAN B

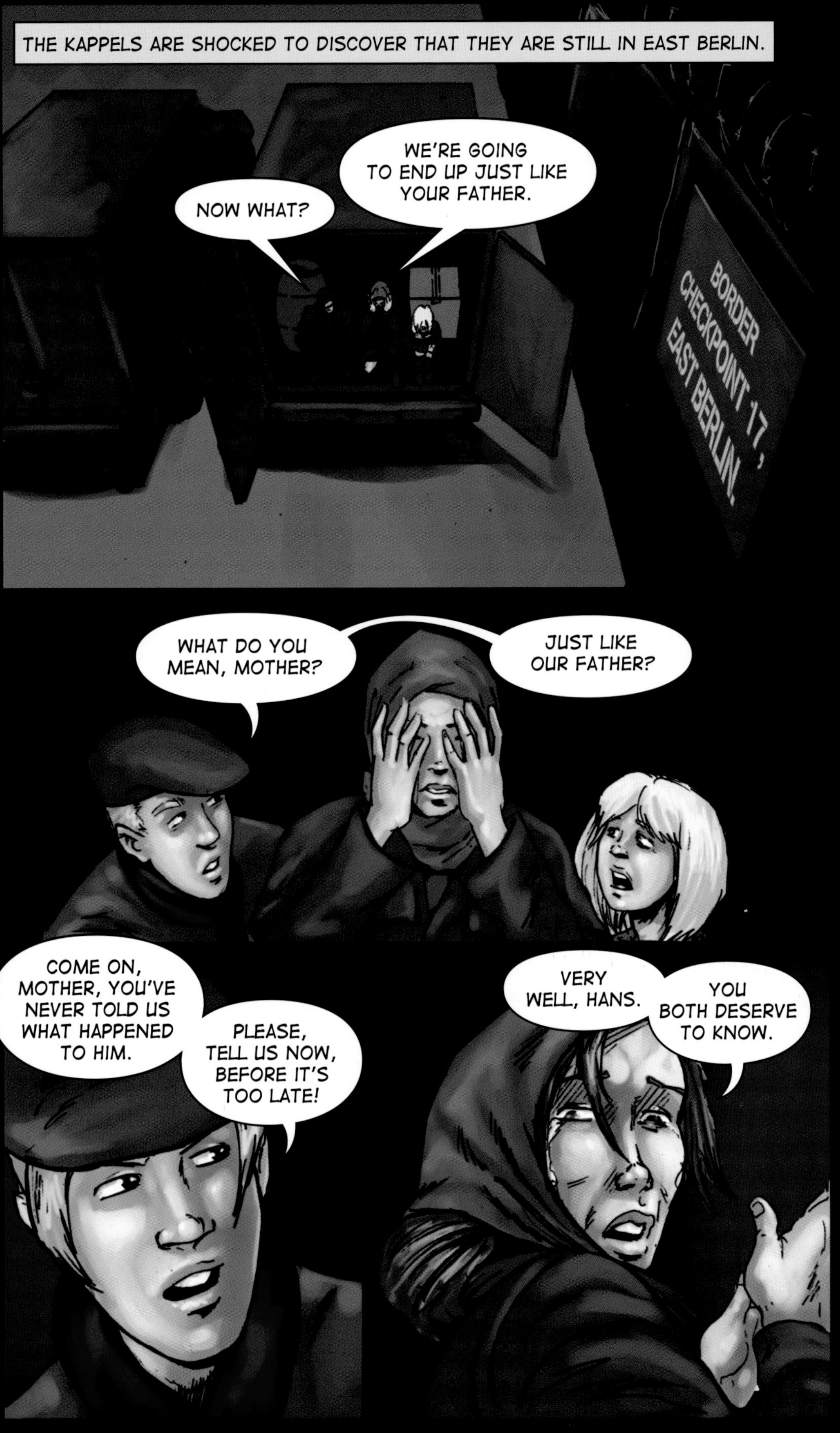

East Berlin police carrying Peter Fechter's body, 1962

THE HUMAN TOLL

While the Wall stood, close to 240 people were killed trying to cross into West Berlin. Imagine how those standing on the west side of the Wall felt when they watched 18-year-old Peter Fechter and his friend, Helmut Kulbeik, trying to escape over the Wall!

Both young men had run across an open area known as the death strip. They were climbing the Wall when Fechter was shot in the hip in front of hundreds of witnesses. Kulbeik made it over, but Fechter fell back down on the eastern side. He desperately cried out for help, but no one on either side of the fence came to his aid.

Fechter bled to death. An hour after he was shot, the guards came out and dragged his body away while the citizens of West Berlin chanted "Murderers!"

A monument to Fechter now stands on the very spot where he fell and later died.

AS HANS FALLS, HIS JACKET GETS CAUGHT ON THE BARBED-WIRE FENCE!

AARGH!

MY ANKLE!

AIIEEEE!

GO, MARTA!

GOTCHA!

GOODBYE, CHILDREN!

C'MON, MOTHER. I'LL CATCH YOU!

JUMP!

WHAT'S SHE DOING? WHY ISN'T SHE COMING?

SHE'S BUYING US TIME. C'MON, MARTA, RUN!

CAROLINE SEES THAT HANS IS IN DANGER.

I MUST DO SOMETHING TO STOP KEITL!

I KNOW!

NO!

DESERTER!

THE EAST GERMAN BORDER GUARDS TURN ON THEIR SEARCHLIGHT.

LOOK FOR THE DESERTER — AND SHOOT!

NO — WAIT!

42

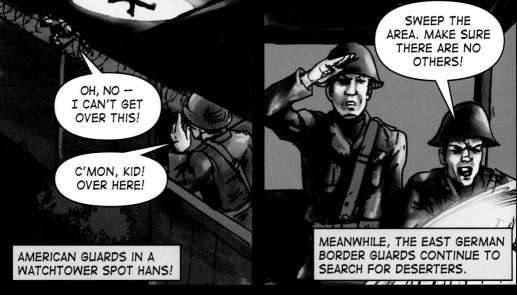

An East Berliner escaping out of her apartment window to the western side of the city, 1961.

GREAT ESCAPES

Many East Berliners were willing to risk their lives to get past the Berlin Wall. About 5,000 people successfully escaped into West Berlin between 1962 and 1989. Climbing the Wall was just one way. There were other clever ways of escape:

TUNNELING

These were often dug by college students, and a whole network of tunnels came to exist underneath East Berlin. The tunnels often began in the basement of a house, in a graveyard, or in an out-of-the-way place. People would follow these tunnels, which ran under the Wall, and escape through to the other side.

FLYING

People tried everything from gliders to hot-air balloons. Two families, the Wetzels and Strlzycks, made it to West Berlin in a homemade balloon. They stitched together pieces of a nylon fabric that they had purchased over a period of time. The sale of lightweight cloth was strictly controlled after this.

OF THE WALL

In November 1989, rumors spread that the East German government would allow travel to West Berlin. This led to a rush at border crossings.

The border guards did not know what to do. Eventually, people had to be allowed through since the government was not willing to shoot them all. East and West Berliners took sledgehammers and other tools to the Berlin Wall. In triumph, they leveled the Wall within a few weeks.

That celebration lasted through 1990, with rock and roll concerts at Potsdamer Platz, a square that had been divided by the Wall. David Hasselhoff, the American singer, actor, and songwriter, performed "Looking for Freedom" from the top of the Berlin Wall. Potsdamer Platz is a must-see place today for tourists and a top shopping area for Berliners.

The fall of the Wall is now a symbol of the end of the Cold War. It was the first step to reuniting Germany.

Crowd at the Brandenburg Gate in Berlin, 1989

INDEX